Romantic
Knitwear

Romantic Knitwear

Maxine Sanford

Arthur Barker Limited
A subsidiary of Weidenfeld (Publishers) Limited

For Ann, Carol and Babs Quinton of Rye
for the years of understanding, patience
and hard work.

My thanks to Gered Mankowitz for his
interpretive photography, Fiona Spencer
for her lucid illustrations and Priory Yarns
of Wakefield for making available to me
their beautiful George Picaud yarns.

Compilation by Doris Bunton
Design by Michael Sedgwick

Published in Great Britain by
Arthur Barker Limited
91 Clapham High Street,
London SW4 7TA

ISBN 0 213 16751 4 cased
      0 213 16757 3 paper

Set, printed and bound in Great Britain by
Fakenham Press Limited, Fakenham,
Norfolk

Contents

General Instructions

Buying yarn To avoid the danger of a mixed dye lot, which will give you a patchy coloured garment, always purchase sufficient yarn to complete the whole design.

Tension First read the whole pattern through very carefully. Using the needle size quoted and the correct yarn, cast on sufficient stitches to obtain a 10 cm (4 in) width. Work in the selected pattern until the work measures 10 cms (4 ins) in length. Cast off. Now measure your square. If it is larger than 10 cms, your tension is too loose and you should try a smaller size needle; if it is too small, then your tension is too tight and you need to use a larger size needle. It is essential to do this tension test before starting any of the patterns in this book.

Sizing Although the patterns are based on an average 91 cms (36 ins) bust size they will in fact fit all sizes from 81–101 cms (32–40 ins). However, if you really want a tighter fit, follow the instructions in the pattern of your choice but use a needle *one size smaller* than stated.

To make buttons (see patterns on pages 24 and 32) Using a 3½ mm crochet hook work in double crochet to form a circle covering the button. Sew firmly at the back.

To make a belt Cut about thirty strands of yarn approximately two metres long. Knot all the strands about 25 cms (9½ ins) from the end and plait in three groups of ten strands until 25 cms from the other end. Knot and brush yarn to make tassles.

Care of your garment Mohair actually improves with washing, provided you wash gently by hand in luke-warm water, using best quality soapflakes and rinsing in Woolite. Lay the garment on a flat surface and pull gently into shape. Mohair garments should not be ironed; if this is necessary use a very cool iron and a damp cloth. It should be folded carefully when dry and aired after each wearing, but do not put it on a hanger.

Abbreviations used in the patterns Needle sizes in round brackets refer to English sizes; those in square brackets refer to American sizes.

alt.	alternate	p.	purl
beg.	beginning	patt.(s)	pattern(s)
cm(s)	centimetre(s)	p.s.s.o.	pass slip-stitch over
dec.	decreas(e)ing	rem.	remain(ing)
foll.	following	rep.	repeating
inc.	increas(e)ing	sl.	slip
in(s)	inch(es)	st.(s)	stitch(es)
k.	knit	t.b.l.	take back loop
m.1.	make one by picking	tog.	together
	up loop between stitches and	y.f	yarn forward
	knitting into the back of it	y.r.n.	yarn round needle

Introduction

The theme of this book is romantic hand-knits. With simplicity as the key and emphasis on glamorous feminine designs which will never date, each garment is unique and flattering to women of all ages.

I have carefully adapted a selection of appropriate designs from my couture collection that are enjoyable to make and sensational to wear. Don't be deterred by the long dresses. They are as easy to make as the tops. You can vary the length of practically all the designs, and details like cuff and collar lengths are best left to your own choice. Experimenting with belts and the lengths of open side seams will enhance the effect of each garment; I have found that a design extending below the hips will make you look slimmer if the side seams are left open up to the waist.

The designs are based on four easy stitches and the yarn used throughout is luxurious mohair. There is a vast range of mohair on the market today, ranging from the pure yarn to 50% mixes – your local wool shop will be able to advise you on the suitability of the various yarns available. Pure mohair is well worth the investment. The word mohair comes from the Turkish 'mukhyar' meaning the 'best or selected' fleece from the Angora goat, and it has been valuable since Biblical times. The Angora goat used to be found exclusively in one province in Turkey but now flourishes in South Africa, South America and Australia as well as the Near East.

Maxine Sanford

Dame du Lac
Dress with Lurex yoke and cuffs

Materials 1,000 grams mohair; 2 reels silver Lurex; a pair each 4 mm (no. 8) [no. 5], 7 mm (no. 2) [no. 10½] and 7½ mm (no. 1) [no. 11] knitting-needles; a cable needle.

Measurements To fit bust 91 to 97 cms (36 to 38 ins); length 147 cms (58 ins); sleeve seam 44 cms (17½ ins).

Tension 8 sts to 5 cms on 7½ mm (no. 2) [no. 10½] needles.

The front * With 7½ mm (no. 1) [no. 11] needles and mohair, cast on 140 sts. Work 4 rows k.1, p.1 rib. Change to 7 mm (no. 2) [no. 10½] needles and patt. as follows: *1st row* K.1 winding yarn twice round needle, (k.1 winding yarn 3 times round needle) to last st., then k.1 winding yarn twice round needle. *2nd row* K.1 dropping off extra loops (sl. next 3 sts on to cable needle and leave at front of work, dropping off extra loops, k.3 sts dropping off extra loops, then k.3 sts from cable needle) to last st., k.1 dropping off extra loops. *3rd and 4th rows* K. to end. These 4 rows form the patt. Rep. them 27 times more, then rep. 1st and 2nd rows once more.

Shape armholes Cast off 6 sts at beg. of next 2 rows. Now work 8 rows patt. dec. 1 st. at both ends of 1st, 3rd and 4th rows each patt. (116 sts). Change to 4 mm (no. 8) [no. 5] needles. *Next row* K.2 tog. to end (58 sts). *Next row* K. to end. Join in Lurex. Using Lurex and mohair tog. cont. as follows: *1st and 2nd rows* (K.1, p.1) to end. *3rd and 4th rows* (P.1, k.1) to end. Rep. the last 4 rows 6 times more.**

Shape neck Rib 21 sts, cast off 16 sts, rib to end. Cont. on last set of sts, dec. 1 st. at neck edge every right side row to 16 sts, ending armhole edge.

Shape shoulder Cast off 8 sts at beg. of next row and foll. alt. row. Join yarns to neck edge of rem. sts and complete to match other side, reversing shapings.

The back Work as front from * to **. Cont. straight in patt. until armholes match front to shoulders.

Shape shoulders Cast off 8 sts at beg. of next 4 rows. Cast off rem. sts.

The sleeves With 4 mm (no. 8) [no. 5] needles and using Lurex and mohair together, cast on 40 sts. Work 17 rows k.1, p.1 rib. *Next row* In rib, inc. in every st. (80 sts). Break Lurex and cont. in mohair only. Change to 7 mm (no. 2) [no. 10½] needles and cont. in main open-work patt. until 8 complete patts. and 1st and 2nd rows of 9th patt. have been worked.

Shape top Cast off 6 sts at beg. of next 2 rows; work 3 more complete patt. dec. 1 st at both ends of 1st, 3rd and 4th rows. Work 4 rows patt., casting off 4 sts at beg. of each row, then k. 2 rows, casting off 4 sts at beg. of each row. Cast off rem. sts.

The neck band Join shoulder seams. You will need an extra needle for this. With 4 mm (no. 8) [no. 5] needles and mohair and right side facing, beg. at centre front neck, pick up and k. 94 sts round neck, ending at centre front. Cont. in rows of k.1, p.1 rib. for 14 rows. Cast off loosely in rib.

To make up Join side and sleeve seams. Sew in sleeves. Fold neckband in half to wrong side and slip-stitch down.

The belt See General Instructions on page 6.

Dame du Lac

Dame du Lac or Lady of the Lake is adapted from my Arthurian collection. It is made in a cross-loop stitch with Lurex on the yoke and cuffs and is an absolutely stunning dress that can be worn as a winter wedding-dress or for special evenings at home. The illustrations show the different ways of wearing it. You can thread the belt through the dress leaving the back free to float which gives it another dimension. A fine body-stocking can be worn underneath.

Demozel

Blouson top

Materials 280 grams mohair; a pair each 7 mm (no. 2) [no. 10½], 5½ mm (no. 5) [no. 8], 5 mm (no. 6) [no. 7] and 3¾ mm (no. 9) [no. 4] knitting-needles; a 4½ mm (no. 7) [no. 1] crochet hook.

Measurements To fit bust 86 to 97 cms (34 to 38 ins); length 53 cms (21 ins); sleeve seam 46 cms (18 ins).

Tension 6 sts to 5 cms on 5½ mm (no. 5) [no. 8] needles.

The back and front (worked alike) With 7 mm (no. 2) [no. 10½] needles, cast on 70 sts. Work 4 rows k.1, t.b.l., p.1 rib. Change to 5½ mm (no. 5) [no. 8] needles and cont. in patt. *Next row* K.2, (y.r.n., p.2 tog.) to last 2 sts, k.2. This row forms the patt. Rep. it until work measures 43 cms.

Shape raglan armhole Cast off 3 sts at beg. of next 2 rows; dec. 1 st. at both ends of next row and foll. alt. rows to 56 sts. Now dec. 1 st. at both ends of every foll. 4th row to 50 sts. Work 3 rows straight after last dec. row. Leave sts on spare needle.

The sleeves With 3¾ mm (no. 9) [no. 4] needles, cast on 40 sts. Work 19 rows k.1, t.b.l., p.1 rib. *Next row* In rib, inc. 1 st. in every st. to end (80 sts). Change to 5½ mm (no. 5) [no. 8] needles and cont. in patt. as back until sleeve measures 46 cms.

Shape top Cast off 3 sts at beg. of next 2 rows; dec. 1 st. at both ends of next row and foll. 3 alt. rows, then at both ends of every foll. 4th row to 60 sts. Work 3 rows straight after last dec. row. Leave sts on spare needle.

The neckband With 5½ mm (no. 5) [no. 8] needles and right side facing, k. across sts of right sleeve, back, left sleeve, then front. *Next row* K.2 tog. to end (110 sts). Change to 5 mm (no. 6) [no. 7] needles and work 4 rows k.1, t.b.l., p.1 rib. Cast off in rib.

To make up Sew in raglan sleeves. Join neckband. Join side and sleeve seams. With crochet hook and using double yarn, make 2 chains 92 cms long. Tie knot at each end leaving ends to form tassels. Thread one through lower edge above ribbing and one at neck.

Demozel

This blouse in a beehive stitch is beautifully practical; not only can you wear it for almost any special occasion but it works very well over a shirt or blouse for the office or any casual activity. It can be worn off the shoulder for evening, belted at the waist, or threaded through the rib to make a full blouson shape. Side seams split to approximately ten inches from the bottom will give a smock effect.

Nineve

Square neck rib and pattern sweater

Materials 200 grams mohair; a pair each 5½mm (no. 5) [no. 8] and 4 mm (no. 8) [no. 5] knitting-needles; a medium size crochet hook.

Measurements To fit bust 86 to 91 cms (34 to 36 ins) length 52 cms (20½ ins); sleeve seam, 41 cms (16 ins).

Tension 7 sts to 5 cms on 5½mm (no. 5) [no. 8] needles.

The back With 5½mm (no. 5) [no. 8] needles, cast on 66 sts and work 2 rows k.1, p.1 rib. Cont. in patt. as follows: *1st row* K.3,* (y.f., k.2 tog.) 3 times, k.3; rep, from * to end. *2nd row* P.3,* (y.r.n., p.2 tog.) 3 times, p.3; rep. from * to end. These 2 rows form the patt. Rep. them until 64 rows have been completed.

Shape armholes Cast off 4 sts at beg. of next 2 rows; dec. 1 st. at both ends of next row and every foll. alt. row until 50 sts rem.** Cont. straight in patt. for 27 rows, ending after wrong side row.

Shape shoulders Cast off 7 sts at beg. of next 4 rows. Change to 4 mm (no. 8) [no. 5] needles and work 5 rows k.1, p.1 rib on rem. sts, dec. 1 st. at both ends of every alt. row. Cast off in rib.

The front Work as back to**.

Shape neck Patt. 17 sts, turn, leave rem. sts on spare needle. Cont. in patt. on 17 sts as follows: *1st row* P.1, y.r.n., p.2 tog. p. 3, patt. to last st., p.1. *2nd row* K.1, patt. as in 1st patt. row above to last 3 sts, then y.f., k.2 tog., k.1. Rep. these 2 rows until work matches back to shoulder, ending armhole edge.

Shape shoulder Cast off 3 sts, then (k.2 tog., cast off 1) 3 times, patt. to end (7 sts). Work 1 row in patt. Cast off rem. sts. With right side facing, sl. 1st 16 sts on to holder and leave for front neck, join yarn to rem. sts and complete to match other side, reversing shapings.

The sleeves With 5½mm (no. 5) [no. 8] needles, cast on 48 sts. Work 2 rows k.1, p.1 rib. Now cont. in main patt. as back for 76 rows.

Shape top Cast off 4 sts at beg. of next 2 rows; dec. 1 st. at both ends of next row and foll. alt. rows to 32 sts. Work 18 rows straight. Dec. 1 st. at both ends of next 7 rows. Cast off rem. sts.

The neck borders Sl. 16 sts at front neck on to 4 mm (no. 8) [no. 5] needle. Work 5 rows k.1, p.1 rib, dec. 1 st. at both ends of alt. rows. Cast off in rib. With right side facing, using 4 mm (no. 8) [no. 5] needles pick up and k.34 sts along right neck edge. Work 5 rows k.1, p.1 rib, dec. at both ends of alt. rows. Cast off. Work left side edge to match.

To make up Join shoulder and neckband seams. Join side and sleeve seams. Sew in sleeves, easing in at top to form slight fullness. Join shaped ends at front neck. With crochet hook and using double yarn make a chain 164 cms long. Tie knot at each end, leaving fringed tassel.

Nineve

Nineve is a quick-to-make little sweater in a beehive and rib stitch. With a crotcheted cord threaded through the bottom, it looks very chic with a tailored skirt or trousers.

Camille

Sweater with pleated collar

Materials 400 grams mohair; a pair each 3¼mm (no. 10) [no. 3], 4 mm (no. 8) [no. 5] and 4½mm (no. 7) [no. 6] knitting-needles; an extra 4 mm (no. 8) [no. 5] needle for collar.

Measurements To fit bust, 91 to 97 cms (36 to 38 ins); length 60 cms (23½ins); sleeve seam 41 cms (16 ins).

Tension 10 sts to 5 cms on 4½mm (no. 7) [no. 6] needles.

The back* With 3¼mm (no. 10) [no. 3] needles, cast on 108 sts. Work 10 rows k.1, p.1 rib. Change to 4½mm (no. 7) [no. 6] needles and patt. as follows: *1st row* P.1, (y.r.n., p.2 tog.) to last st., p.1. This row forms the patt. Rep. it until work measures 36 cms.

Shape armholes *1st row* K.1, k.2 tog., patt. to last 3 sts, k.2 tog., k.1. *2nd row* K.1, patt. to last st., k.1. Rep. 2nd row twice more. Now rep. the last 4 rows 6 times more.** Rep. 1st and 2nd rows until 56 sts rem.

Shape shoulders Cast off 12 sts at beg. of next 2 rows. Leave rem. 32 sts on spare needle.

The front Work as back from * to **. Now rep. 1st and 2nd rows of armhole shaping until 74 sts rem.

Shape neck K.2 tog., patt. until 30 sts are on right-hand needle, turn, leave rem. sts on spare needle. Cont. on 1st set of sts thus: *Next two rows* K.2 tog., patt. to end. Rep. these 2 rows until 15 sts rem. Now keeping neck edge straight cont. dec. at armhole edge on alt. rows to 12 sts. Cast off. With right side facing, sl. 12 sts at front on to spare needle and leave for front neck. Join yarn to rem. sts and complete to match other side.

The sleeves With 3¼mm (no. 10) [no. 3] needles, cast on 56 sts. Work 16 rows k.1, p.1 rib, inc. 4 sts evenly along last row. Change to 4½mm (no. 7) [no. 6] needles and cont. in main patt. as back, inc. 1 st. at both ends of 9th row and every foll. 8th row to 76 sts. Cont. straight until sleeve measures 41 cms.

Shape top Rep. the first 4 rows of back armhole shaping twice, then rep. 1st and 2nd rows until 16 sts rem. Work 8 rows straight. Leave sts on spare needle.

The collar With 3¼mm (no. 10) [no. 3] needles and wrong side facing, k. across 16 sts on right sleeve, pick up and k. 14 sts down right neck edge, k. across 12 sts at centre front, pick up and k. 15 sts along left neck edge, k. across 16 sts on left sleeve, k. across 32 sts at back neck (105 sts). Cont. as follows: *1st row* K.1 (p.1, k.1) to end. *2nd row* P.1 (k.1, p.1) to end. Rep. last 2 rows 4 times more, than 1st row once. *1st inc. row* P.1 (k.1, m.1, p.1) to end (157 sts). *Next row* (K.2, p.1) to last st., k.1. *Next row* P.1 (k.1, p.2) to end. Work 5 more rows in rib as set. *2nd inc. row* P.1 (k.1, m.1., p.2) to end (209 sts). *Next row* (K.3, p.1) to last st., k.1. *Next row* P.1 (k.1, p.3) to end. Change to 4 mm (no. 8) [no. 5] needles and work 3 more rows rib as set. *3rd inc. row* P.1 (k.1, m.1., p.3) to end (261 sts). *Next row* (K.4, p.1) to last st., k.1. *Next row* P.1 (k.1, p.4) to end. Work 3 more rows rib as set. On next inc. row you will need your extra needle. *4th inc. row* P.1 (m.1., k.1, m.1., p.4) to end (365 sts). *Next row* (K.4, p.3) to last st., k.1. *5th inc. row* P.1 (m.1., k.3, m.1., p.4) to end (469 sts). *Next row* (K.4, p.5) to last st., k.1. *6th inc. row* P.1 (m.1., k.5, m.1., p.4) to end (573 sts). *Next row* (K.4, p.7) to last st., k.1. *Next row* K. to end. Cast off.

To make up Sew in raglan sleeves and flat stitch collar. Join side and sleeve seams.

Camille

Inspired by *The Lady of the Camellias* and knitted in a beehive stitch this top can be worn on or off the shoulder. It is blatantly feminine and can look very sexy or charmingly demure (see opposite), depending on how you wear it.

Kristina
Cossack sweater or dress

Materials For sweater, 240 grams mohair; for dress, 960 grams mohair; a pair each 6½mm (no. 3) [no. 10] and 3¾mm (no. 9) [no. 4] knitting-needles; a cable needle; 3 small buttons.
Measurements To fit bust 86 to 91 cms (34 to 36 ins); length of sweater 64 cms (25 ins); length of dress 138 cms (54 ins); sleeve seam 43 cms (17 ins).
Tension 6 sts to 4 cms on 6½mm (no. 3) [no. 10] needles.

THE SWEATER
The back With 6½mm (no. 3) [no. 10] needles, cast on 74 sts. Work 4 rows k.1, p.1 rib. Change to patt. as follows: *1st row* K.1 winding yarn twice round needle (k.1 winding yarn 3 times round needle) to last st., k.1 winding yarn twice round needle. *2nd row* K.1 dropping off extra loops (sl. next 3 sts on to cable needle and leave at front of work, dropping off extra loops, k.3 sts, dropping off extra loops, then k.3 sts from cable needle) to last st., k.1 dropping off extra loops. *3rd and 4th rows* K. to end. These 4 rows form the patt. Rep. them until 13 complete patts. and 1st and 2nd rows of 14th patt. have been worked.
Shape armholes Cast off 4 sts at beg. of next 2 rows; then work 8 rows patt., dec. 1 st. at both ends of 1st row and every foll. alt. row. Work 10 rows patt.
Shape shoulders Cast off 8 sts at beg. of next 4 rows. Leave rem. 26 sts on spare needle.

The front Work as for back until armhole shapings are completed (58 sts).
Divide for front opening Patt. 30 sts, turn, leave rem. sts on spare needle. *Next row* Patt. to end. Work 6 more rows in patt. on these 30 sts. *Next row* Patt. to last 8 sts, turn, leave these sts on safety-pin. Cast off 3 sts at neck edge on next row and foll. alt. row.
Shape shoulders Cast off 8 sts at beg. of next row and foll. alt. row. With right side facing, sl. first 8 sts from spare needle on to holder and leave for front band. Join yarn to rem. 20 sts and work 8 rows patt., ending at neck edge. Cast off 2 sts at beg. of next row and foll. alt. row. Work 2 rows patt., thus ending at armhole edge. Shape shoulders as for back.

The front band Sl. 8 sts from holder on to 3¾mm (no. 9) [no. 4] needle, join yarn and work in k.1, p.1 rib until band will fit up front opening. Cont. in rib, dec. 1 st. at neck edge on every row until all sts are worked off. With 3¾mm (no. 9) [no. 4] needles, cast on 8 sts for button band. Dec. 1 st. at inner edge of every row until all sts are worked off.

The sleeves With 3¾mm (no. 9) [no. 4] needles, cast on 40 sts. Work in k.1, p.1 rib for 19 rows. *Next row* Inc. in every st. to end. Change to 6½mm (no. 3) [no. 10] needles and cont. in main patt. on these 80 sts until 10 complete patts have been worked. Now work 1st and 2nd row of next patt.
Shape top Cast off 4 sts at beg. of next 2 rows. Dec. 1 st. at both ends of next row and foll. alt. rows to 28 sts. Cast off 8 sts at beg. of next 4 rows. Cast off rem. sts.

Kristina

THE DRESS

The back and front (worked alike) With 6½mm (no. 3) [no. 10] needles, cast on 74 sts. Work 4 rows k.1, p.1 rib. Now cont. in main patt. until 1st and 2nd rows of 31st patt. from beg. have been worked. Complete as sweater from armholes. Work sleeves as sweater.

The belt See General Instructions on page 6.

To make up Join shoulders, side and sleeve seams on the sweater. Sew in sleeves, any fullness to top. Sew on front bands.

The collar With 3¾mm (no. 9) [no. 4] needles and right side facing, pick up and k.68 sts round neck, including sts on spare needle and safety-pin. Work 30 rows k.1, p.1 rib. Cast off loosely in rib. Fold collar in half and slip-stitch on wrong side. Sew on buttons – these will easily push through top front band, so no buttonholes are required.

Adapted from the Russian style and made in a cross-loop stitch, this is one of the most versatile garments. It can be worn as a thigh-length top which looks stunning with trousers or as a glamorous long dress for the evening. You can make the splits as daring as the photograph on page 25 or to the length that you desire. A fine body-stocking can be worn underneath.

Sophie
Dropped stitch square neck sweater

Materials 280 grams mohair; a pair each 5½ mm (no. 5) [no. 8], 5 mm (no. 6) [no. 7] and 4 mm (no. 8) [no. 5] knitting-needles; a 4 mm (no. 12) crochet hook.

Measurements To fit bust 91 to 97 cms (36 to 38 ins); length 63 cms (24½ ins); sleeve seam 45 cms (17½ ins).

Tension 8 sts to 5 cms over pattern on 5 mm (no. 6) [no. 7] knitting-needles.

The back *With 5½ mm (no. 5) [no. 8] knitting-needles, cast on 70 sts. Work 4 rows k.1, t.b.1., p.1 rib. Change to 5 mm (no. 6) [no. 7] needles and cont. in patt. as follows:
1st row (wrong side) K.1, winding yarn twice round needle, to end. *2nd row* P., dropping off extra loops from previous row. *3rd row* P. *4th row* K. These 4 rows form the patt. Rep. them 16 times more (i.e. 64 rows), then rep. 1st and 2nd rows once.
Shape armholes Cast off 6 sts at beg. of next 2 rows. Work 2 rows straight. Dec. 1 st. at both ends of next 2 rows.** Work straight for 5 complete patts, then 1st and 2nd patt. rows once.
Shape shoulders Cast off 7 sts at beg. of next 4 rows. Cast off rem. sts.

The front Work as back from * to **.
Shape neck Patt. 14 sts, cast off 26, patt. to end. Cont. in patt. on 1st set of sts until work matches back to shoulder, ending armhole edge.
Shape shoulders Cast off 7 sts at beg. of next row and foll. alt. row. With right side facing, join yarn to neck edge of rem. sts. and complete to match other side.

The sleeves With 4 mm (no. 8) [no. 5] needles, cast on 40 sts. Work 19 rows k.1, t.b.1, p.1 rib. *Next row* Work in rib, inc. in every st. (80 sts). Change to 5 mm (no. 6) [no. 7] needles and cont. in patt. until 2nd row of 17th patt. from beg. has been worked.
Shape top Work 5 complete patts. dec. 1 st. at both ends of next row (3rd patt. row) and every foll. alt. row. Cast off 5 sts at beg. of next 8 rows. Cast off rem. sts.

To make up Join shoulder, side and sleeve seams. Set in sleeves. With 4 mm (no. 12) crochet hook and right side facing, work 1 row double chain all round neck. Fasten off.

Sophie

This pretty sweater in an easy drop stitch looks casual with jeans and a shirt or, belted and worn with boots, gives you the full Russian flavour.

Mitsuka

Mandarin-style jacket

Materials 300 grams mohair; a pair each $5\frac{1}{2}$mm (no. 5) [no. 8] and $4\frac{1}{2}$mm (no. 7) [no. 6] knitting-needles.

Measurements To fit 91 to 97 cms (36 to 38 ins); length 60 cms ($23\frac{1}{2}$ ins); sleeve seam 43 cms (17 ins).

Tension 7 sts to 5 cms on $5\frac{1}{2}$mm (no. 5) [no. 8] needles.

The back With $5\frac{1}{2}$mm (no. 5) [no. 8] needles, cast on 68 sts. Work 10 rows k.1, t.b.1., p.1 rib. Cont. in main patt. as follows: *1st row* K.1, (y.f., sl.1, k.1, p.s.s.o.) to last st.; k.1. This row forms the patt. Rep. it 69 times more.

Shape armholes Dec. 1 st. at both ends of next row. Work 3 rows straight. Rep. last 4 rows twice more. Now dec. 1 st. at both ends of next row and every foll. alt. row to 34 sts, ending after a wrong side row.

Shape shoulders Cast off 6 sts at beg. of next 2 rows. Leave rem. 22 sts on spare needle.

The left front With $5\frac{1}{2}$mm (no. 5) [no. 8] needles, cast on 44 sts. Work 10 rows k.1, t.b.1., p.1 rib. Cont. in patt. as follows: *1st row* Work in patt. as back to last 11 sts., p.1, then (k.1, t.b.1., p.1) 5 times. *2nd row* (K.1, t.b.1., p.1) 5 times, patt. to end. Cont. in patt. keeping 10 sts at front edge in twisted rib until work matches back to armhole, ending at side edge.

Shape armhole Keeping front edge straight dec. at armhole edge as back to 32 sts, ending at front edge.

Shape neck Cast off 10 sts at beg. of next row. Cont. dec. at armhole edge on alt. rows as before, at the same time dec. 1 st. at neck edge every row to 6 sts. Work 1 row. Cast off.

The right front Work as left front, reversing position of twisted rib (k.1, t.b.1., p.1) front band and shapings.

If buttonholes are required, work as follows: on 2nd row of right front band, cast off the 2 central sts, then rib to end. *Next row* Cast on 2 sts over cast-off sts. Repeat every 8 cms (3 ins) up front band.

The sleeves With $5\frac{1}{2}$mm (no. 5) [no. 8] needles, cast on 52 sts. Work 10 rows twisted rib (k.1, t.b.1., p.1). Cont. in main patt. for 76 rows.

Shape top Dec. 1 st. at both ends of next 6 rows, then dec. 1 st. at both ends of next row and foll. alt. rows to 8 sts. Work 3 rows straight, and leave sts on spare needle.

The neckband With $4\frac{1}{2}$mm (no. 7) [no. 6] needles and right side facing, beg. inside 10 sts from right front edge. Pick up and k. 19 sts to shoulder, k. across sts on right sleeve, back neck and left sleeve, pick up and k. 19 sts down left neck edge, ending inside 10 sts from left front edge (76 sts). Work 20 rows k.1, t.b.1., p.1 rib. Cast off in rib.

To make up Sew in sleeves. Join side and sleeve seams. Fold neckband in half to wrong side and slip-stitch down. Sew on buttons if desired.

Mitsuka

A mandarin-style jacket made in a beehive stitch, useful for all occasions either as a snugly-fitting jacket or loose over a blouse or dress. Buttons are optional with this design.

Katerina

Ribbed yoke sweater

Materials 320 grams mohair; a pair each 6½mm (no. 3) [no. 10], 5½mm (no. 5) [no. 8] and 4½mm (no. 7) [no. 6] knitting-needles; a set of double pointed 4½mm (no. 7) [no. 6] knitting-needles.

Measurements To fit bust, 86 to 97 cms (34 to 38 ins); length 62 cms (24½ ins); sleeve seam 46 cms (18 ins).

Tension. 4 sts and 4 rows to 3 cms over patt. on 6½mm (no. 3) [no. 10] needles.

The back With 5½mm (no. 5) [no. 8] needles, cast on 70 sts. Work 14 rows k.1, t.b.l., p.1 rib. Change to 6½mm (no. 3) [no. 10] needles and patt. as follows: *1st row* K.1, (y.r.n., p.2 tog.) to last st., k.1. This row forms the patt. Rep. it 53 times more.

Shape armholes Keeping patt. correct. cast off 6 sts at beg. of next 2 rows; dec. 1 st. at both ends of next row and foll. alt. rows to 54 sts. Work 1 row after last dec. row. Change to 4½mm (no. 7) [no. 6] needles and work in k.1, t.b.l., p. 1 rib for 42 rows.

Shape shoulders Cast off 7 sts at beg. of next 4 rows; leave rem. 26 sts on spare needle.

The front Work as for back until 32 rows twisted rib have been worked for yoke.

Shape neck Patt. 19 sts, turn, leave rem. sts on spare needle. Cont. on 1st set of sts, dec. 1 st. at neck edge on next row and every foll. alt. row to 14 sts, ending armhole edge.

Shape shoulder Cast off 7 sts at beg. of next row and foll. alt. row. With right side facing, sl. 1st 16 sts on to spare needle and leave for front neck, join yarn to rem. 19 sts and complete to match other side.

The sleeves With 4½mm (no. 7) [no. 6] needles, cast on 40 sts. Work 19 rows k.1, t.b.l., p.1 rib. *Next row* In rib, inc. in every st. (80 sts). Change to 6½mm (no. 3) [no. 10] needles and cont. in main patt. as back for 58 rows.

Shape top. Cast off 6 sts at beg. of next 2 rows; dec. 1 st. at both ends of next row and foll. alt. rows to 58 sts, ending after a wrong side row. Cast off 6 sts at beg. of next 6 rows. Cast off rem. sts.

To make up Join shoulder, side and sleeve seams. Sew in sleeves.

The collar With set of 4½mm (no. 7) [no. 6] needles and right side facing beg. at centre front rib across 8 sts on spare needle, pick up and k. 72 sts round neck, then rib across 8 sts at front. Work in rows of k.1, t.b.l., p.1 rib for 22 rows. Cast off in rib. Fold neckband in half to right side and slip stitch down.

Katerina

A soft, dreamy top in a beehive stitch
which can be worn with jeans or more
formally with a skirt. It can be split at the
sides if desired, or worn as a
blouse-sweater with an Oriental look.

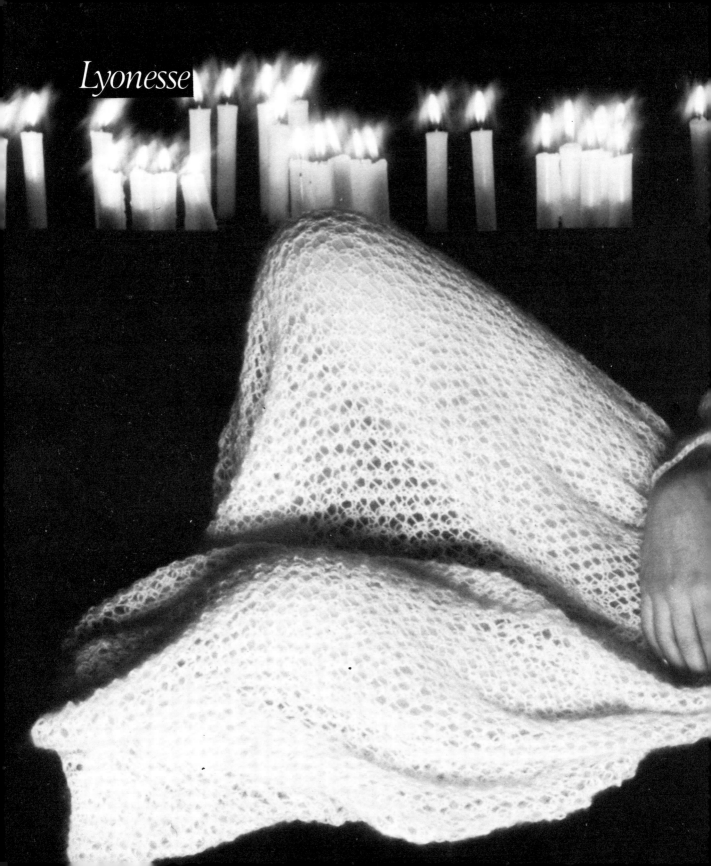

Lyonesse

Lyonesse
V-neck sweater or dress

Materials For sweater, 250 grams mohair; for dress, 500 grams mohair; a pair each $2\frac{3}{4}$ mm (no. 12) [no. 1] and 5 mm (no. 6) [no. 7] knitting-needles.

Measurements To fit bust 81 to 91 cms (32 to 36 ins); length of top 51 cms (20 ins); length of dress 148 cms (58 ins); sleeve seam 44 cms ($17\frac{1}{2}$ ins).

Tension 10 sts to 5 cms on 5 mm (no. 6) [no. 7] needles.

THE SWEATER

The back and front (worked alike) With $2\frac{3}{4}$ mm (no. 12) [no. 1] needles, cast on 68 sts. Work 34 rows k.1, p.1 rib. Change to 5 mm (no. 6) [no. 7] needles and cont. as follows: *1st row* K. 34 sts, turn, leave rem. sts on spare needle. *2nd row* K. to end. Cont. on these 34 sts in patt. as follows: *1st and 2nd rows* K.1, then (y.f., k.2 tog.) to last st., k.1. *3rd and 4th rows* K. These 4 rows form the patt. Rep. them 3 times more, at the same time dec. at front edge on next (5th) row and every foll. 6th row (32 sts).

Shape armhole Still dec. at front edge every 6th row, cast off 3 sts at beg. of next row, then dec. at armhole edge every 4th row to 8 sts. Cast off. With right side facing, join yarn to rem. sts and complete to match other side, reversing shapings.

The front bands (2) Join shoulder seams. With $2\frac{3}{4}$ mm (no. 12) [no. 1] needles, cast on 8 sts. Work in k.1, p.1 rib until the band, slightly stretched, will fit up shaped front edge, over shoulder and down back, ending at top of ribbing. Cast off.

The sleeves With $2\frac{3}{4}$ mm (no. 12) [no. 1] needles, cast on 40 sts. Work 33 rows k.1, p.1 rib. *Next row* Inc. in each st. to end (80 sts). Change to 5 mm (no. 6) [no. 7] needles and rep. the patt. rows until 15 complete patts. have been worked.

Shape top Cast off 3 sts at beg. of next 2 rows; dec. 1 st. at both ends of next row and foll. alt. rows to 38 sts, then at both ends of every row to 4 sts. Cast off.

To make up Join side and sleeve seams. Sew in sleeves. Sew on front bands, crossing right over left and catching down at top of rib.

THE DRESS

The back and front (worked alike) With 5 mm (no. 6) [no. 7] needles, cast on 136 sts. Work 4 rows k.1, p.1 rib. Now rep. the 4 patt. rows as sweater until work measures 97 cms (38 ins), ending on 3rd patt. row. *Next row* K.2 tog. to end (68 sts). Change to $2\frac{3}{4}$ mm (no. 12) [no. 1] needles and cont. as for sweater to end.

To make up As top, joining skirt seam to lower edge.

THE HAT

Make a plait about 1 cm ($\frac{3}{8}$ in) thick to go round your head. Make two smaller plaits to run from the back of the head to the front and sew them on about 2 ins apart; then do two more small plaits and sew them on to go across the first two (see previous page). Make several plaits long enough to hang to your waist and attach them to the thick plait, working from one side round the back to the other side.

Inspired by the medieval Queen Eleanor of
Aquitaine, this is quite a daring dress and
you've got to be bold to wear it – but if you
do I guarantee you'll turn a few heads. The
dress in the photograph on page 41 was
knitted in George Picaud's King Mohair
which creates a particularly light effect; a
slightly thicker dress will be obtained with
other brands of mohair. It works well with
a fine body-stocking.

Zelda
Jacket with shawl collar

Materials 320 grams mohair; a pair each 4 mm (no. 8) [no. 5], 5½ mm (no. 5) [no. 8] and 3¾ mm (no. 9) [no. 4] knitting-needles.

Measurements To fit bust 86 to 91 cms (34 to 36 ins); length 66 cms (26 ins); sleeve seam 43 cms (17 ins).

Tension 8 sts to 5 cms on 5½ mm (no. 5) [no. 8] needles.

The back With 5½ mm (no. 5) [no. 8] needles, cast on 72 sts. Work 6 rows k.1, t.b.l., p.1 rib, inc. 1 st. at end of last row (73 sts). Cont. in patt. as follows: *1st row* K.1, (y.f., sl.1., k.2 tog., p.s.s.o., y.f., k.1) to end. *2nd row* P to end. These 2 rows form the patt. Rep. them until 76 rows in all have been completed.

Shape raglan armhole Keeping patt. correct and counting sts when dec. cast off 2 sts at beg. of next 2 rows. Dec. 1 st. at both ends of next row. Work 3 rows straight. Now dec. 1 st. at both ends of next row and foll. alt. rows to 23 sts. Cast off.

The left front With 5½ mm (no. 5) [no. 8] needles, cast on 42 sts. Work 6 rows k.1, t.b.l., p.1 rib inc. 1 st. at end of last row. Cont. on these 43 sts. as follows: *1st row* Patt. to last 6 sts, then (k.1, t.b.l., p.1) 3 times. *2nd row* (K.1, t.b.l., p.1) 3 times, then patt. to end. Rep. last 2 rows until work matches back to armhole, ending after 2nd row.

Shape raglan armhole Cast off 2 sts at beg. of next row. Work 1 row. Dec. 1 st. at beg. of next row and every foll. alt. row to 31 sts, ending at front edge. *Next row* Rib 6 sts, leave these on safety-pin. P.2 tog., p. to end. Still dec. at raglan as before, dec. 1 st. at neck edge every foll. alt. row until 4 sts rem. Keeping neck edge straight, dec. at armhole edge until all sts are worked off.

The right front. Work to match left front, reversing shapings and position of ribbed border.

The sleeves With 4 mm (no. 8) [no. 5] needles, cast on 40 sts. Work 19 rows k.1, t.b.l., p.1 rib. *Next row* Rib 3, inc. in next st., (rib 1, inc. in next st.) 16 times, rib to end (57 sts). Change to 5½ mm (no. 5) [no. 8] needles and cont. in patt. as back until sleeve measures 43 cms, ending after 2nd row.

Shape top Keeping patt. correct and counting sts when dec., cast off 2 sts at beg. of next 2 rows. Dec. 1 st. at both ends of next row. Work 3 rows straight. Now dec. 1 st. at both ends of next row and every foll. alt. row to 7 sts. Cast off.

To make up Sew in raglan sleeves. Beg. 27 cms up from lower edge join side seams, then sleeve seams.

The collar Sl. 6 sts of left front on to 5½ mm (no. 5) [no. 8] needle, join on yarn and work in twisted rib (k.1, t.b.l., p. 1) inc. 1 st. at end, outer edge on next row and every foll. alt. row until collar will fit up front, across sleeve top, to centre back neck. Cast off. Work other side to match. Flat st. cast-off edges tog. Then sew collar to neck.

The belt With 3¾ mm (no. 9) [no. 4] needles, cast on 12 sts. Work 144 cms k.1, t.b.l., p.1, rib. Cast off in rib.

Zelda

Made up in a beehive stitch with shawl
collar, fitted sleeves and knitted belt, this is
a jacket which suits everybody and can be
worn anywhere, any time.

Natasha

Ribbed yoke sweater

Materials 320 grams mohair; a pair each 3¼mm (no. 10) [no. 3] and 5mm (no. 6) [no. 7] knitting-needles.

Measurements Bust 91 cms (36 ins); length 61 cms (24 ins); sleeve seam 46 cms (18 ins).

Tension 8 sts to 5 cms over pattern on 5mm (no. 6) [no. 7] needles.

The back and front (worked alike) With 3¼mm (no. 10) [no. 3] needles, cast on 100 sts. Work 21 rows k.1, t.b.l., p.1 rib, inc. 1 st. at both ends of last row (102 sts). Change to 5mm (no. 6) [no. 7] needles and cont. in patt. as follows: *1st row* (K.2, y.f., sl.1, k.1, p.s.s.o.) to last 2 sts, then k.2. *2nd row* (P.2, y.r.n., p. 2. tog.) to last 2 sts, then p. 2. These 2 rows form the patt. Rep. them until work measures 41 cms, ending after 2nd patt. row.
Shape armholes Cast off 3 sts at beg. of next 2 rows; dec. 1 st. at both ends of next row and foll. alt. row. Work 1 row, thus ending after wrong side row. Leave sts on spare needle.

The sleeves With 3¼mm (no. 10) [no. 3] needles, cast on 48 sts. Work 21 rows k.1, t.b.l., p.1 rib. *Next row* Rib 3, * inc. in next st., rep. from * to last 3 sts, rib to end (90 sts). Change to 5mm (no. 6) [no. 7] needles and cont. in patt. as back until work measures 46 cms, ending after 2nd patt. row.
Shape top Cast off 3 sts at beg. of next 2 rows; dec. 1 st. at both ends of next row and foll. alt. row. Work 1 row. Leave sts on spare needle.

The yoke With 5mm (no. 6) [no. 7] needles and right sides facing, k. across 80 sts of left sleeve top, 92 sts of front, 80 sts of right sleeve, 92 sts of back (344 sts). *Next row* P. to end. Cont. as follows: *1st row* P.1 (k.2, t.b.l., p.2) to last 3 sts, then k.2, t.b.l., p.1. *2nd row* K.1 (p.2, k.2, t.b.l.) to last 3 sts, then p.2, k.1, t.b.l. Rep. last 2 rows 3 times. *1st dec. row* P.1 (k.2, t.b.l., p.2 tog., k.2, t.b.l., p.2) to last 7 sts, then k.2, t.b.l., p.2 tog., k.2, t.b.l., p.1 (301 sts). Keeping rib correct as set work 11 rows as above. *2nd dec. row* P.1 (k.2, t.b.l., p.1, k.2, t.b.l., p.2 tog.) to last 6 sts, then k.2, t.b.l., p.1, k.2, t.b.l., p.1 (259 sts). Work 7 rows rib as now set. *3rd dec. row* P.1 (k.2 tog., t.b.l., p.1, k.2, t.b.l., p.1) to last 6 sts, then k.2 tog., t.b.l., p.1, k.2, t.b.l., p.1 (216 sts). Work 5 rows rib as now set. *4th dec. row* P.1 (k.1, t.b.l., p.1, k.2 tog., t.b.l., p.1) to last 5 sts, then k.1, t.b.l., p.1, k.2 tog., t.b.l., p.1 (173 sts). Work 3 rows rib as now set. *5th dec. row* P.1, k.1, t.b.l., (p.1, k.1, t.b.l., p.1, k.3 tog., t.b.l.) to last 3 sts, then p.1, k.1, t.b.l., p.1 (117 sts). *6th dec. row* K.1, t.b.l., p.1 (k.3 tog., t.b.l., p.1, k.1, t.b.l., p.1) to last 7 sts, then k.3 tog., t.b.l., p.1, k.1, t.b.l., p.2 tog. (78 sts). Change to 3¼mm (no. 10) [no. 3] needles and work 18 rows twisted rib (k.1, t.b.l., p.1). Cast off in rib.

To make up Join back yoke from neck to beg. of rib. Join side and sleeve seams. Sew in underarm sleeves. Fold neckband in half to wrong side and slip-stitch down.

Natasha

The design of this sweater has a very luxurious and individual look. The yoke cascades from the small turtle neck into a combination of rib and beehive stitch. This sweater with its cosy elegance is a must for everyone.

Muschka

Bolero

Materials 300 grams mohair; a pair each 4½ mm (no. 7) [no. 6] and 5½ mm (no. 5) [no. 8] knitting-needles.

Measurements To fit bust 86 to 91 cms (34 to 36 ins); length 61 cms (24 ins); sleeve seam 44 cms (17½ ins).

Tension 8 sts to 5 cms over pattern on 5½ mm (no. 5) [no. 8] knitting-needles.

The back With 4½ mm (no. 7) [no. 6] needles, cast on 92 sts. Work 7 rows k.2, t.b.l., p.2 rib. *Next row* Change to 5½ mm (no. 5) [no. 8] needles and k.5, k.2 tog. (k.4, k.2 tog.) to last 7 sts, k. to end (78 sts). Cont. in patt. as follows: *1st row* (right side) P.2, (y.r.n., p.2 tog., p.2) to end. *2nd row* K.2 (y.f., s.1, k.1, p.s.s.o., k.2) to end. These 2 rows form the patt. Rep. them until 70 patt. rows in all have been completed.

Shape armholes Cast off 3 sts at beg. of next 2 rows; dec. 1 st. at both ends of every row to 66 sts, then at both ends of alt. rows to 62 sts. Work straight in patt. for 33 rows.

Shape shoulders Cast off 5 sts at beg. of next 2 rows; 6 sts at beg. of foll. 4 rows. Cast off rem. sts.

The right front With 5½ mm (no. 5) [no. 8] needles cast on 22 sts and k. 1 row. Beg. in main patt. as back inc. 1 st. at beg. of 1st row and 1 st. at the end (same edge) on 2nd row. Rep. last 2 rows 8 times more (32 sts). Keeping patt. correct inc. 1 st. at same edge every alt. row to 38 sts. Work straight in patt. for 22 rows thus ending at front edge. Now shape front by dec. 1 st. at beg. of next row and at this edge every foll. 5th row to 32 sts, ending at front edge. Work 1 row.

Shape armhole Cast off 3 sts at beg. of next row. Cont. dec. at front edge on foll. 3rd row and every foll. 5th row, *at the same time* dec. 1 st. at armhole edge on next 3 rows, then on foll. 2 alt. rows. Keeping armhole edge straight cont. to dec. at front edge as before to 17 sts. Cont. straight until armhole matches back to shoulder, ending armhole edge.

Shape shoulder Cast off 5 sts at beg. of next row, 6 sts on foll. 2 alt. rows.

The left front Work to match right front, reversing shapings.

The sleeves With 4½ mm (no. 7) [no. 6] needles, cast on 38 sts. Work 11 rows k.2, t.b.l., p.2 rib. Change to 5½ mm (no. 5) [no. 8] needles. *Next row* K.2 (inc. in next st., k.2) to end (50 sts). Beg. with 1st row, cont. in main patt. as back, inc. 1 st. at both ends of 11th row and every foll. 12th row to 62 sts working inc. sts into patt. as available. Cont. straight until sleeve measures 44 cms, ending after 2nd patt. row.

Shape top Cast off 3 sts at beg. of next 2 rows; dec. 1 st. at both ends of every row to 46 sts, then every alt. row to 30 sts, then every row to 18 sts. Cast off.

The front band With 4½ mm (no. 7) [no. 6] needles, cast on 228 sts. Work 8 rows k.2, t.b.l., p.2, rib. Cast off in rib.

To make up Join shoulder seams. Sew on front band beg. at left side edge, easing in at rounded portion, up front and across back neck, then down other side, ending at right side edge. Join side and sleeve seams. Sew in sleeves.

Muschka

This fun bolero in a beehive stitch is quick
to make and doubles as a waistcoat or
evening jacket.

Sylphide

Deep V sweater

Materials 400 grams mohair; a pair each 4 mm (no. 8) [no. 5] and 6 mm (no. 4) [no. 9] knitting-needles.

Measurements To fit bust 86 to 97 cms (34 to 38 ins); length 67 cms (26½ ins); sleeve seam 46 cms (18 ins).

Tension 7 sts to 5 cms on 6 mm (no. 4) [no. 9] needles.

The back With 4 mm (no. 8) [no. 5] needles, cast on 62 sts. Work 20 rows k.1, t.b.l., p.1 rib, inc. 12 sts evenly along last row (74 sts). Change to 6 mm (no. 4) [no. 9] needles and patt. as follows: *1st row* K.2 (y.f., k.2 tog.) to last 2 sts, k.2. This row forms the patt. Rep. it for 55 more rows (36 cms).

Shape raglan armhole Cast off 1 st. at beg. of next 2 rows; dec. 1 st. at both ends of next row and every foll. alt. row to 20 sts. Cast off.

The front Work as for back until front measures 26 cms from beg. (36 patt. rows).

Divide for front opening Patt. 34 sts, turn, cast on 6 sts, turn. Cont. on these 40 sts as follows: *1st row* (K.1, t.b.l., p.1) 3 times then patt. to end. *2nd row* Patt. to last 6 sts (k.1, t.b.l., p.1) 3 times. Cont. as set with 6 sts at neck edge in twisted rib and rem. sts in patt. Dec. 1 st. inside ribbed border on foll. 4th row then every foll. 6th row until work matches back to armhole. End at side edge.

Shape raglan armhole Still dec. at neck edge every 6th row as before, at the same time, cast off 1 st. at armhole edge on next row, then dec. 1 st. at same edge every right side row until 15 sts rem. Keeping neck edge straight cont. to dec. at armhole edge as before until 6 rib sts rem. Leave sts on spare needle. With right side facing, join yarn to inner edge of rem. sts. *1st row* (K.1, t.b.l., p.1) 3 times, then patt. to end. Complete to match other side, reversing shapings.

The sleeves With 4 mm (no. 8) [no. 5] needles, cast on 32 sts. Work 25 rows k.1, t.b.l., p.1 rib. *Next row* (K.1, inc. in next st.) to last st., k.1 (62 sts). Change to 6 mm (no. 4) [no. 9] needles and cont. in main patt. until sleeve measures 46 cms.

Shape top Work as back to 8 sts. Cast off.

To make up Sew in sleeves. Join side and sleeve seams. Sl. 6 sts at right neck edge on to 6 mm (no. 4) [no. 9] needles and work in twisted rib (k.1, t.b.l., p.1) until long enough to fit across sleeve top and across to centre back neck. Cast off. Work left side to match. Join back seam, then sew band across sleeve tops and back neck.

Sylphide

With its deep plunging neckline and raglan
sleeves, this sweater can be worn as a
quick throwover with a shirt or as a
practical cover-up worn in the formal style
of the illustration opposite.

Guinevere

Long dress

Materials 960 grams mohair; a pair each 7½ mm (no. 1) [no. 11], 6½ mm (no. 3) [no. 10] and 4 mm (no. 8) [no. 5] knitting-needles.

Measurements To fit bust 86 to 91 cms (34 to 36 ins); length 132 cms (52 ins); sleeve seam 46 cms (18 ins).

Tension 7 sts to 5 cms on 6½ mm (no. 3) [no. 10] needles.

The back and front (worked alike) With 7½ mm (no. 1) [no. 11] needles, cast on 138 sts and work 2 rows k.1, p.1 rib. Change to 6½ mm (no. 3) [no. 10] needles and cont. in patt. as follows: *1st row* K.1 (k.2 tog., y.f.) to last st., then k.1. This row forms the patt. Rep. it until work measures 110 cms.

Shape raglan armholes * *1st row* Cast off 3 sts, k.1 (k.2 tog., y.f.) to last st., then k.1. *2nd row* Cast off 3 sts, y.f. (k.2 tog., y.f.) to last 2 sts, then k.2. *3rd row* K.2 tog., y.f., to last 4 sts, then k.2 tog. twice. ** Now rep. 3rd row until 86 sts rem. Leave sts on spare needle.

The sleeves With 4 mm (no. 8) [no. 5] needles, cast on 40 sts. Work 19 rows k.1, t.b.l., p.1 rib. *Next row* In rib inc. in every st. (80 sts). Change to 6½ mm (no. 3) [no. 10] needles and cont. in main patt. for front and back until sleeve measures 46 cms.

Shape top Work as for front and back raglan shaping from * to **. Then rep. 3rd row until 28 sts rem. Leave sts on spare needle.

The neckband With 6½ mm (no. 3) [no. 10] needles and wrong side facing, k. across sts of right sleeve, front, left sleeve and back (228 sts). *Next row* K.2 tog. to end (114 sts). Change to 4 mm (no. 8) [no. 5] needles and work 8 rows k.1, t.b.l., p.1 rib. Cast off in rib.

To make up Join raglan seams and neckband. Join side and sleeve seams.

Guinevere

Adapted from the Arthurian collection,
this flowing dress has a medieval feeling.
To be worn by the fire through the autumn
into the deep winter, it has all the drama of
Arthur's court. Ideally a fine body-stocking
should be worn underneath.